Fermented Foods vol. 3: Water Kefir

Written by Meghan Grande

Book 3 of **The Food Preservation Series** of Books

Disclaimer:

The information contained in this book is for general information purposes only.

While we endeavor to keep the information up to date and correct, we make no representations or warranties of any kind, express or implied, about the completeness, accuracy, reliability, suitability or availability with respect to the book or the information, products, services, or related graphics contained in the book for any purpose. Any reliance you place on such information is therefore strictly at your own risk.

None of the information in this this book is meant to be construed as medical advice. Always consult with a medical profession prior to making any dietary changes in your life.

This book is about fermented beverages. The author of the book is not a trained professional in food safety or any related field. Neither the author nor the publisher is responsible for any damages arising from the use or misuse of the information provided in this book.

Contents

Introduction

This is the third book of this series. I wasn't sure how the first two books were going to be received, but so far they've exceeded my expectations and have been every bit as popular as I hoped they would be. The first volume covered fermenting vegetables and the second took on milk kefir. It only makes sense that the third volume would roll right into water kefir, which is similar to kefir in that probiotic grains are used for fermentation, but differs in the types of grains used, the abilities of the grains and the way the kefir tastes.

The first time I tried water kefir, I had no idea what to expect. To put it mildly, I wasn't impressed. I tried my kefir as soon as it was done fermenting, without adding any sort of flavoring to it, and found it to taste exactly the way you'd expect fermented sugar water to taste. It was heavy and thick and tasted like fermented syrup. I couldn't imagine it being good with any amount of flavoring and ended up dumping the entire batch down the drain.

I didn't try water kefir again for months.

I may not have ever tried it again were it not for a friend who convinced me to take a sip of her strawberry-infused fizzy water kefir. It was like night and day compared to my original experience. This water kefir was the polar opposite of the kefir I'd made. It was light and fizzy, with a pleasant strawberry scent and taste that perfectly complimented the kefir. I was hooked.

I relentlessly plied my friend for all of her water kefir secrets and realized I'd made a few basic mistakes the first time I'd tried to make it. Too much sugar, too short of a ferment and drinking the kefir without adding anything to it were all factors that contributed to the off-putting initial experience. I soon learned how to make good water kefir and have been enjoying it for years.

Once you learn the ropes, water kefir is easy to make. Don't let a bad initial experience ruin it for you like I almost did. I've heard water kefir described as a lightly-carbonated, completely natural soda and that's a pretty good description of what good water kefir tastes like. If you miss the mark, switch things up a bit and try again. Water kefir is inexpensive to make, so throwing out a batch or two before you get it right isn't going to break the bank.

What is Water Kefir?

Water kefir is a probiotic beverage made by placing grains known as water kefir grains into sugary liquid and allowing them to ferment the liquid. The end result is a beverage that's packed with probiotic cultures that can be used as a base to make a number of other drinks.

When water kefir grains are added to a liquid containing sugars, the lactobacteria and yeasts in the grains go to work. They feed on the sugar in the liquid, converting it to lactic acid, alcohol and carbon dioxide gas. This creates a beverage that lightly-sweetened, full of probiotic bacteria and is either lightly-effervescent or carbonated, depending on how long the kefir is fermented for.

Don't be fooled by the term "lacto" in lactobacteria. Water kefir contains no lactose, so it's a great choice for lactose-intolerant individuals looking to avoid the lactose found in milk kefir and other fermented milk products. It's also gluten-free, has a low glycemic load and is low in calories, making it a good choice for diet-conscious individuals.

The bacterial profile of water kefir isn't quite as robust as that of milk kefir, but you still get a pretty good dose of probiotics. You can make up the difference by drinking more water kefir, which is easy because it's light and isn't as thick as milk kefir.

What Are Water Kefir Grains?

Water kefir grains are made up of a symbiotic matrix of bacteria and yeasts held together by polysaccharides emitted by the bacteria. They almost look crystalline, but feel rubbery to the touch.

While it's widely believed the original milk kefir grains came from the Caucuses Mountain region that separates Russia from Georgia, the exact origin of water kefir grains isn't known. One popular theory is the original grains were found growing inside prickly pear cactuses in Mexico. I've also read that legend has it the original grains were gifted to Mother Teresa by Tibetan monks (1).

When you take into consideration the fact that water kefir grains are used by various cultures spanning the globe, it's likely the grains came from multiple sources and there is no single original source from which all the grains grew. This becomes even more likely when you realize the grains are composed of different combinations of bacteria and yeasts depending on where in the world they're found.

Regardless of where in the world you find them, they all have one thing in common. They can be used time and time again to ferment sugary liquids into probiotic beverages. When properly cared for and fed, water kefir grains will last indefinitely and may even start to grow.

Probiotics in Water Kefir

A number of strains of lactobacteria and yeasts are known to exist in water kefir grains. Here are just some of the many probiotic cultures known to exist in water kefir:

- *A wide variety of yeasts.*
- *Bacillus graveolus.*
- *Bacillus subtilus.*
- ***Lactobacillus acidophilus.***
- *Lactobacillus alactosus.*
- ***Lactobacillus brevis.***
- *Lactobacillus bulgaricus.*
- ***Lactobacillus casei.***
- *Lactobacillus coryneformis.*
- *Lactobacillus fructosus.*
- ***Lactobacillus hilgardii.***
- *Lactobacillus hordei.*
- ***Lactobacillus kefiri.***
- *Lactobacillus nagelii.*
- ***Lactobacillus plantarum.***
- *Lactobacillus pseudoplantarum.*
- *Leuconostoc citreum.*
- ***Leuconostoc mesenteroides.***
- *Pediococcus damnosus.*
- *Streptococcus agalactiae.*
- *Streptococcus bovis.*
- *Streptococcus cremeris.*
- *Streptococcus lactis.*

- *Streptococcus pyogenes.*

There are a handful of bacteria and yeasts that are shared between water kefir grains and milk kefir grains. The bacteria on the list that are highlighted in bold are shared by both milk kefir and water kefir. Consuming both milk kefir and water kefir will give you a wider array of probiotics than consuming one or the other.

The Health Benefits of Water Kefir

There have been quite a few studies done of late on milk kefir, but water kefir hasn't garnered the same attention. What is known is water kefir contains a wide variety of probiotic bacteria. One study found 453 different bacterial isolates, with the vast majority of them being lactobacteria (2).

Probiotic bacteria help the body in a number of ways. Their main duty is keeping the gut healthy by helping to digest foods and fight off harmful pathogens that enter the gut. Bacteria outnumber human cells in the body 10 to 1 and are vital to ensuring the body functions at a high level (3). As these bacteria die off due to both external and internal factors, they need to be replaced. The Western diet is largely devoid of probiotic bacteria, which can result in imbalances in the gut. When the good bacteria disappear, there are harmful bacteria lurking in the wings, waiting for their opportunity to step in and take over. If this is allowed to happen the consequences can be severe.

Probiotic bacteria aren't just good for your gut and digestive health, they're tied in to the rest of the body in ways scientists are just now starting to understand. When the gut is unhealthy, the immune system starts to break down and problems can arise all over the body. Keeping your gut healthy is important because it allows your body to focus its immune response on the areas that need it instead of having to dedicate valuable resources to keeping the gut healthy.

While not all of the benefits have been scientifically documented, there are quite a few health benefits believed to be associated with consumption of water kefir. Here are some the benefits people claim to have gained from drinking this tasty elixir:

- **Allergy relief, both from minor food allergies and seasonal allergies.** Never attempt to use water kefir to treat major food allergies.
- **Better absorption of vitamins and minerals.**
- **Better gut health.**
- **Detoxification of the body.**
- **Improved digestion.**
- **Improved immune system health.**
- **Improved overall health.**
- **Lower cholesterol.**
- **Weight loss, due to the intestinal flora being able to better process food.**

One of the biggest benefits we've realized in our household is we've used water kefir to completely eliminate soda pop from our diets. Instead of the high fructose corn syrup, artificial flavors and colors and other harmful ingredients found in soda, we're drinking water kefir in its place. That alone is reason enough for me to fall in love with kefir all over again.

How Much Water Kefir Should You Drink?

Water kefir contains probiotic cultures and it contains a bunch of them, so it's best to start off slow. This is especially important if you've been eating a diet that's largely devoid of probiotic cultures and aren't sure about the health of your gut.

Consuming probiotic foods may initiate what's known as a *die-off*, in which the bad bacteria in the gut start to die in large amounts as the probiotic bacteria you're consuming start to crowd them out. The dying bacteria release toxins as they die, which isn't a problem when small amounts of bacteria are dying, but can make you feel sick when large amounts of bacteria all start to die off at once.

Start with a few sips of water kefir and go from there. If you drink a small amount and feel fine, increase the amount you drink the next time around. Each time you drink it, add a little more until you're at a level you're comfortable with. If you start to feel sick or rundown, back off to a lesser amount and allow your body time to adjust. You don't want to chug a full glass of water kefir the first time you drink it and accidentally set a huge die-off in motion. If you're lucky, there won't be any long-term health effects from a die-off, but you aren't going to feel very good in the short-term.

Easing into water kefir (or any other probiotic food or drink, for that matter) is best done under the guidance of a physician, who should be able to help you determine whether any side effects you're suffering are a result of a die-off or some other health concern. Your physician should also be able to help you determine how much water kefir you can safely consume daily. It's powerful stuff and isn't one-size-fits-all.

Keeping Your Grains Healthy

Water kefir grains are largely a product of their environment, so it's important to take the necessary steps to keep them in good health. Keep your grains happy and healthy and you'll be rewarded with batch after batch of water kefir, as your grains continue to produce indefinitely. With a little care, your first water kefir grain purchase could be the only grains you'll ever have to buy.

Most, but not all, sets of healthy water kefir grains will produce new grains as they ferment kefir. This shouldn't be your sole determinant of grain health, as there is the occasional set of grains that works fine for fermenting, but is stubborn when it comes to producing new grains. If you've tried everything and can't get your grains to reproduce, you may have to replace them in order to get grains that are willing to grow.

The key to keeping your grains healthy is to keep them fed. Water kefir grains require sugar water and they need it often. For best results, switch the grains to new sugar water every 24 to 48 hours. This will ensure they have plenty of food and are capable of working to their maximum ability. You have to be careful what sort of sugars you're feeding your grains, as they prefer sucrose to other types of sugar.

While raw honey is a healthy choice for most other recipes, it's generally avoided in water kefir recipes because the honey can damage water kefir grains over time. If you do want to add honey to water kefir, add the honey after the grains have been removed.

Water kefir grains do well when fed natural sugars like rapadura and molasses that contain minerals. If you're using white sugar, you should add a pinch of unrefined sea salt to the fermenting vessel in order to ensure the mineral needs of the grains are met.

Some recipes call for placing water kefir grains in fruit juices or other acidic liquids. The grains will ferment the juice, but they may start to struggle after a while. You might be able to bring struggling grains back by switching them to sugar water. If you decide to ferment juices, keep a set of backup grains handy in case your grains get damaged beyond repair.

Heat can impact the speed at which water kefir grains process sugar. When temperatures start to climb, water kefir grains speed up and the water they're in will need to be switched out more often. If you're storing your grains in a warm area of the house, you might have to switch the sugar water they're in every 24 hours. Water kefir grains do best when fermented in a room with an ambient temperature between 65° F and 78° F. You may be able to ferment kefir outside of this range, but you aren't doing the grains any favors.

Why Is There So Much Sugar?

One of the first things health-conscious people notice about water kefir recipes is the large amount of sugar that's used during a water kefir ferment. Most recipes call for a quarter cup of sugar per quart of water used in the recipe. This is especially problematic when the recipe calls for white sugar, which most healthy individuals avoid at all costs.

For most people, there's little to worry about when it comes to the sugar added prior to fermentation because most of it is consumed by the lactobacteria and yeasts in during fermentation. The enzymes released during fermentation break the sugars down into simple sugars that are easy for the body to digest and don't cause an increase in blood sugar. The exact amount of sugar left varies from ferment to ferment and is largely dependent on the length of the ferment, but there's often less than 20% of the sugar you started with in the final product.

Diabetics and others who are sensitive to sugar should consult with their primary care provider prior to consuming water kefir. Some diabetics are reportedly able to handle it, but that's a decision you should make after talking to your doctor.

What Type of Sugar Works Best?

Water kefir grains are highly-individual and their needs may differ from culture to culture and possibly even season to season. We've found natural sugars that contain trace amounts of minerals seem to work best for our grains. Others have reported white sugar mixed with a tablespoon or two of molasses works best. Don't be afraid to experiment with various sugar types and combinations of sugars until you find the one that works the best for your grains.

The following sugars can all be used to ferment water kefir:

- **Brown sugar.**
- **Cane sugar.**
- **Demarara.**
- **Jaggery.**
- **Maple syrup.**
- **Molasses.**
- **Muscavado.**
- **Palm sugar.**
- **Powdered sugar.**
- **Raw sugar.**
- **Sucanat.**
- **Turbinado.**
- **White sugar.**

Artificial sweeteners won't work because they don't contain the sucrose the bacteria need to feed on. Attempting to use artificial sugars can starve your grains and may do irreparable damage.

We mentioned honey briefly in an earlier chapter, but it bears mention again. Honey is not a good option for water kefir because it has natural antibiotic properties. Water kefir grains can use the sugars in honey to ferment kefir, but the repeated use of honey may weaken them over time. I compare it to a human being fed water contaminated with mercury. It won't kill you right away, but will gradually slow you down until you can barely function. There are tons of other options, so it's best to avoid honey altogether.

Alcohol in Water Kefir

One of the biggest reservations some people have regarding water kefir is the alcohol content. While there is some alcohol in water kefir because of the fermentation process, the amount of alcohol is usually fairly low. Shorter ferments typically contain less than 1% alcohol, while longer ferments may creep a little bit higher than that.

Keep in mind that more sugar will equal more alcohol in the final product, especially if it's left to ferment for a longer period of time. Use sugar in moderation and shoot for lightly-sweet kefir instead of trying to create something as sweet as the sodas you're used to.

I'm often asked if water kefir is OK to give to children. That's a decision you'll have to make on your own, but I will tell you this. I've given it to my children and they've never gotten drunk from drinking a small glass of water kefir or eating a kefir popsicle. I think the small amount of alcohol in the kefir isn't a problem when you consider the probiotic cultures and other benefits they're gaining.

The Fermenting Jar: Anaerobic vs. Aerobic Fermenting

Aerobic fermenting is fermenting done in an environment into which air can freely enter. This sort of fermenting is usually done with a loose cloth or cheesecloth cover secured over the top of the fermenting jar. *Anaerobic fermenting* is done in an environment in which air is prevented from getting into a container, usually through use of airlock containers.

There is a significant amount of debate going on as to the best type of container to use for fermenting water kefir. Some fermenters use traditional fermenting methods, in which pretty much any non-reactive container can be used as long as a breathable cover can be placed over it. Others will only use airlock containers, which are anaerobic containers that allow pressure to be released from the container while keeping oxygen from entering, because they claim they're safer and mold and harmful bacteria are less likely to grow in an airtight fermenting environment.

Water kefir has been fermented in an aerobic environment with loose covers (or no cover at all) for quite some time and you rarely find a person who claims to have fallen ill from drinking water kefir. I'm sure it's happened, as mishandling any food item can allow harmful pathogens to develop, but properly-fermenting water kefir creates an environment in which harmful pathogens will have a tough time growing.

In my opinion, airlock containers aren't the absolute necessity some people are claiming they are. They are convenient and do work well for fermenting water kefir, so they can be used if you'd like. They may also be marginally safer, as they will prevent certain pathogens from developing. One nice thing about airlock containers is they automatically off-gas the container, so you don't have to worry about opening the container periodically to release pressure. For many, this convenience alone is reason enough to use airlock containers.

The Fermenting Jar: What Material Should It Be Made Of?

The vast majority of people fermenting water kefir do so in a glass container. Some use mason jars or canning jars. Others use glass bottles. Yet another subset uses glass jars with fancy airlock lids attached to them. While there's much debate as to the necessity of anaerobic vs. aerobic fermenting, there's little debate as to the best type of container material.

Fermenting can be done in other types of containers, but there's little reason to do so. Glass is a good choice because it's non-reactive and won't react to the acids created during the fermenting process. It's non-porous and doesn't contain any nooks and crannies in which harmful pathogens can hide and grow. Glass is also inexpensive and glass jars can be purchased from most grocery and department stores.

Plastic containers can be used for fermenting, but I avoid them because of the possibility of chemicals leaching out of the plastic. Yes, there are food-grade plastics that supposedly don't leach chemicals, but I still don't trust them. Ceramic containers may contain lead in the glaze. Wooden containers are to be avoided because they have small ridges and holes that can trap tiny food particles and harbor the wrong types of bacteria.

Go with glass and you won't have any of the worries you do with the other container types.

Storing Water Kefir Grains

Buying grains and fermenting your own water kefir is a commitment that ties up quite a bit of your time. Active kefir grains have to be moved into a new batch of sugar water every couple of days when you're making kefir for consumption. At most, they'll last 5 days in a container of sugar water before they start to really struggle.

There may come a time in your life when you find you don't have the time to properly care for your grains and need to store them for safekeeping. Instead of tossing them out or neglecting them and leaving them to die, store them using one of the following methods generally thought to be safe for placing water kefir grains into suspended animation:

- **Store them in the fridge.** Grains stored in the fridge in an airtight container of sugar water will last up to a month. Swap the sugar water out every couple weeks.
- **Freeze the grains.** For longer-term storage, rinse the grains off and freeze them. They should last a few months in the freezer.
- **Dehydrate the grains.** Water kefir grains can be dried by setting them out at room temperature for a few days or by using a dehydrator set to its lowest setting. Dehydrated grains will last indefinitely, but the longer they're stored, the less likely they are to come back to life.

There's a good chance you're going to lose some of the grains when you freeze or dehydrate them, so always store more than you think you're going to need. That way you'll have enough grains to account for any losses you may suffer.

Rehydrating Dried Grains

Some manufacturers dehydrate water kefir grains before they ship them out. This stabilizes the grains and allows them to be shipped long distances without having to worry about the grains running out of food while in transit. If you purchase dehydrated grains, you're going to have to rehydrate them before using them to make water kefir.

Rehydration is a fairly easy process. Here are the supplies you're going to need to gather in order to rehydrate your grains:

- **Dehydrated water kefir grains.**
- **A quart of mineral or spring water.** Don't use fluoridated tap water or water that's been filtered using a method that eliminates natural minerals. Chlorinated tap water can be used, but boil it for 30 minutes to get rid of the chlorine.
- **5 tablespoons of sugar.** Rapadura, coconut sugar or maple syrup will all get the job done. If using white sugar, add a tablespoon or two of molasses to the jar.
- **A glass jar.**
- **A mesh strainer.** You'll want a fine mesh strainer made of plastic to filter the grains out of the kefir.
- **A wooden or plastic spoon.** Don't use metal, as certain metals can damage water kefir grains. Some sources say stainless steel is acceptable, but you're better off using wood or plastic.

- **A thin towel or some cheesecloth.** This will be used to cover the jar to ensure insects, dirt and dust can't get in.
- **Twine or a rubber band.** This will be used to secure the cover in place.

Follow these steps to rehydrate your grains:

1. Gently warm the water in a saucepan on the stove. Add the sugar to the water and stir it in until it's dissolved.
2. Place the water into the jar and give it time to cool to room temperature before moving on to step 3.
3. Once the water is cool, add the kefir grains to the water and use the spoon to stir the contents of the jar.
4. Cover the jar with a towel or a piece of cheesecloth and secure it in place.
5. Let the mixture sit for 3 days at room temperature. This should be long enough to rehydrate the grains. After 3 days have passed, strain the grains out of the liquid and discard the liquid. The grains should be rubbery to the touch and have fattened up nicely. If not, follow steps 1 through 5 again.
6. If the grains look good, test them by attempting to make a batch of water kefir. If the water kefir is good, you're all set. If not, the grains may level out and start producing good kefir after a few more ferments.

Most sets of dehydrated grains are able to be rehydrated after a single 3-day ferment, but there is the occasional stubborn batch that takes up to a month to get going. Keep swapping out the sugar water every 2 to 3 days and watch for signs the grains are coming back to life.

When all else fails, contact the person or company you bought the grains from. They may have some tips to help you restore your grains to their former glory.

How to Make Plain Water Kefir

You should learn to make plain water kefir before you try making other varieties. It's easier to figure out the type and amount of sugar to use when there's nothing else in the jar. Practice makes perfect, so work on this recipe until you get it right.

Here are a couple tips to help you on your way:

- **Longer ferments equal less sugar in the final product.** A 24-hour ferment will contain more sugar than a 48-hour ferment and will therefore have a sweeter taste. Some people prefer the sweeter taste of a short ferment, while others prefer fermenting most of the sugar out of the kefir.

- **Longer ferments mean more alcohol.** Most water kefir ferments result in kefir with less than 1% alcohol, but be aware the longer you ferment kefir, the more alcohol it'll contain.

- **Longer ferments mean more carbon dioxide.** Carbon dioxide gives water kefir an effervescent mouthfeel. It's similar to drinking a lightly-carbonated soda. There's a trick to getting more carbonation that we'll cover in the next chapter.

- **The golden ratio is ¼ cup of sugar and ¼ cup of water kefir grains to every quart of water you're fermenting, but all grains have different requirements.** Start with this ratio and adjust the amount of grains you're adding until the kefir is just right.

You'll need the same supplies you needed when rehydrating your grains. To recap, here are the supplies you're going to need:

- ¼ cup water kefir grains.
- A quart of mineral or spring water.
- ¼ cup of the sugar or sugar blend of your choice.
- A glass jar.
- A mesh strainer.
- A wooden or plastic spoon.
- A thin towel or some cheesecloth.
- Twine or a rubber band.

Follow these directions to make basic water kefir:

1. Heat up the water and stir the sugar into it until it dissolves.
2. Pour the sugar water into the jar and let it cool.
3. Add the kefir grains to the jar.
4. Cover the jar with the towel or cheesecloth and secure the cover in place.
5. Ferment the water kefir at room temperature for 24 to 48 hours.
6. Once the kefir has fermented to your preference, strain the grains out of the kefir and move them to a new container of sugar water.
7. Store the kefir in an airtight container in the fridge.

You can taste this water kefir if you'd like, but you aren't likely to enjoy it in its current form. Water kefir doesn't start to come into its own until it has had some sort of flavoring added to it.

How to Make Fizzy Water Kefir

Here's another water kefir base recipe you're going to need to know how to make. This recipe creates carbonated water kefir that can be used to make kefir sodas and other carbonated beverages. The longer you leave the kefir to ferment, the more carbonation it'll have, but don't ferment it with the grains in it for more than 72 hours.

The key to making carbonated water kefir is to do what's known as a *second ferment*. This is an additional fermentation period of 24 to 48 hours, done without the grains and with an airtight lid on the jar.

Placing a tight lid onto the jar allows the carbon dioxide gases to build up inside the jar and in the water kefir. Be aware a lot of pressure can build up in the jar during the second ferment. Cover the jar with a towel when you unscrew the lid or you could end up spraying water kefir all over your kitchen. I've never done this with water kefir, but have had it happen while fermenting vegetables and it can make a huge mess. To be safe, set the jar in the sink, place a towel over it and slowly unscrew the lid. Any spray from the jar will be caught in the towel and anything that drips down the sides will land in the sink.

Specialty lids with rubber gaskets can be purchased to help ease the pressure in the jar. These lids will prevent the lid from popping off the jar and making a huge mess if too much pressure builds up. Instead of popping the lid, the gasket expands and relieves some of the pressure. The kefir may shoot out when you open the jar, so you're still going to want to open it in the sink.

In order to make fizzy water kefir, you're going to need the following supplies:

- **¼ cup water kefir grains.**
- **A quart of mineral or spring water.**
- **¼ cup of the sugar or sugar blend of your choice.**
- **A glass jar that can be sealed airtight.**
- **A mesh strainer.**
- **A wooden or plastic spoon.**
- **A thin towel or some cheesecloth.**
- **Twine or a rubber band.**

Notice there's one key difference between this list and the items you need to make plain water kefir. You now need a jar that can be sealed airtight. Other than that, everything else is the same.

Follow these directions to make fizzy water kefir:

1. Warm up the water and stir the sugar into it until the sugar dissolves.
2. Add the water to the fermenting jar and let it cool.
3. Add the water kefir grains to the jar and stir them in.
4. Place a cloth lid on the jar and let it ferment at room temperature for 24 to 48 hours.
5. Remove the grains from the jar and transfer them to another batch of sugar water.
6. Place an airtight lid on the jar and set it out to ferment for an additional 24 to 48 hours. The

longer the ferment, the more carbonation the water kefir should have.

7. Store the water kefir in an airtight container in the fridge when it's done fermenting.

Like plain kefir, unflavored fizzy kefir isn't very good on its own. Adding flavors to fizzy water kefir creates carbonated beverages that are pretty close to soda pop in flavor and effervescence.

Traditional Water Kefir

Traditional water kefir is made by adding a lemon, a dried fig and a piece of dried fruit to regular water kefir before you ferment it. I use dried apricots, but you can use most dried fruit varieties to good effect—just make sure you're using unsulfured fruit that hasn't had anything added to it.

Adding these three ingredients makes water kefir that's surprisingly drinkable.

Ingredients:

1 quart spring or mineral.
¼ cup water kefir grains.
¼ cup of the sugar of your choice.
1 lemon, sliced.
1 dried fig.
A small handful of dried apricots.

Directions:

1. Warm the water and stir the sugar into it until it dissolves.
2. Pour the sugar water into the jar and give it time to cool.
3. Add the rest of the ingredients to the jar and stir them up.
4. Place a towel or a piece of cheesecloth over the mouth of the jar and secure it in place.

5. Ferment the water kefir at room temperature for 24 to 48 hours.

6. Remove the lemon, dried fig and dried apricots from the jar. Strain the water kefir grains out of the kefir and start another ferment with the grains.

7. Store the water kefir in an airtight container in the fridge.

Cultured Lemonade

After trying cultured lemonade, you may never want to go back to drinking traditional lemonade again. Fermenting does something special to lemonade and makes it taste fantastic. Depending on how long the lemonade is fermented, you might need to add a bit of sugar when you drink it. I like my lemonade tart, so I rarely feel the need to add sugar.

Cultured lemonade does well as a plain kefir ferment and also makes fantastic fizzy kefir. Try it both ways to see which you like the best.

Ingredients:

1 quart spring or mineral.
¼ cup water kefir grains.
¼ cup of the sugar of your choice.
¼ cup fresh lemon juice.

Plain Cultured Lemonade Directions:

1. Warm the water and stir the sugar into it until it dissolves. Place the water into the jar and let it cool. Add the water kefir grains to the jar and loosely cover it with a towel or piece of cheesecloth. Secure the cover in place.
2. Ferment the water kefir for 24 hours at room temperature.
3. Strain out the kefir grains.

4. Add the lemon juice to the kefir and stir it in. Taste and add sugar, as needed.
5. Store in an airtight container in the fridge.

Fizzy Cultured Lemonade Directions:

1. Follow steps 1 through 3 of the plain cultured lemonade directions.
2. Add the lemon juice to the fermenting jar and a couple tablespoons of sugar and stir them in.
3. Place an airtight lid on the jar. Ferment the water kefir for an additional 12 to 24 hours, or until it is carbonated to your preference.
4. Move the jar to the fridge when the kefir is ready. Don't forget to off-gas the container.

Strawberry Mint Cultured Lemonade

Eliminate the mint if you want strawberry lemonade. I've subbed both blackberries and raspberries for the strawberries to good effect. This recipe works as either a fizzy beverage or a plain beverage.

Ingredients:

1 quart spring or mineral.
¼ cup water kefir grains.
¼ cup of the sugar of your choice.
¼ cup fresh lemon juice.
1 cup fresh strawberries.
¼ cup mint leaves.

Plain Strawberry Mint Cultured Lemonade Directions:

1. Make plain water kefir and ferment it for 24 hours at room temperature.
2. Strain out the kefir grains.
3. Add the lemon juice to the kefir and stir it in. Taste and add sugar, as needed.
4. Place the strawberries and mint leaves into a blender and blend into a puree.
5. Stir the puree into the kefir.
6. Store it in an airtight container in the fridge.

Fizzy Strawberry Mint Cultured Lemonade Directions:

1. Follow steps 1 through 5 of the previous directions.
2. Place an airtight lid on the container and ferment it at room temperature for an additional 12 to 24 hours.
3. Off-gas the container and move it to the fridge once it's carbonated to your preference.

Lemon-Lime Kefir

As with the other lemonade recipes, this one works as both plain kefir and fizzy kefir. If you time moving your fizzy kefir to the fridge just right, it'll end up tasting just like lemon-lime soda.

Ingredients:

1 quart spring or mineral water.
¼ cup water kefir grains.
¼ cup of the sugar of your choice.
¼ cup fresh lemon juice.
¼ cup fresh lime juice

Lemon-Lime Kefir Directions:

1. Make plain water kefir and ferment it for 24 hours at room temperature.
2. Strain out the kefir grains.
3. Add the lemon and lime juice to the kefir and stir it in. Taste and add sugar, as needed.
4. Store it in an airtight container in the fridge.

Fizzy Lemon-Lime Kefir Directions:

1. Follow steps 1 through 3 of the previous directions.
2. Add a couple tablespoons of sugar to the kefir and stir it in.

3. Place an airtight lid on the container and ferment it at room temperature for an additional 12 to 24 hours.

4. Off-gas the container and move it to the fridge once it's carbonated to your preference.

Cherry-Lime Kefir

Cherry-lime kefir is my go-to kefir when I'm looking to introduce someone to water kefir. Ferment it twice and you'll end up with a carbonated beverage that's light, refreshing and will give any commercial soda out there a run for its money when it comes to flavor. When you consider it's good for you instead of being a contributing factor to a number of health concerns, you've got good reason to switch to water kefir right away.

Use ripe cherries that are a deep red color for best results. The sweetness of the cherries adds depth to the recipe and this kefir just isn't the same when slightly green cherries are used.

Ingredients:

1 quart spring or mineral water.
¼ cup water kefir grains.
¼ cup of the sugar of your choice.
¼ cup fresh lime juice.
½ cup cherries, pitted.

Cherry-Lime Kefir Directions:

1. Make plain water kefir and ferment it for 24 hours at room temperature.
2. Strain out the kefir grains.
3. Blend the cherries and add them to the fermenting vessel. Add the lime juice and stir it in. Taste and add sugar, as needed.

4. Store in an airtight container in the fridge.

Fizzy Cherry-Lime Kefir Directions:

1. Follow steps 1 and 2 of the previous directions.
2. Blend the cherries and add them to the fermenting vessel. Stir the lime juice into the kefir.
3. Place an airtight lid on the container and ferment it at room temperature for an additional 12 to 24 hours.
4. Strain out the cherries and move the kefir to the fridge once it's carbonated to your preference. Be careful when opening the jar after the second ferment. This recipe likes to get really fizzy.

Cherry-Lime Kefir Gelatin

If you're like me and eliminated regular Jello from your diet years ago because of all the sugar, here's a great way to add it back. Once you've tried kefir gelatin, you're never going to want regular gelatin again.

This recipe uses cherry-lime kefir to make gelatin, but it'll work with most of the other fruity water kefir recipes in the book.

Ingredients:

1 quart spring or mineral water.
¼ cup water kefir grains.
¼ cup of the sugar of your choice.
4 tablespoons gelatin.
½ cup fresh lime juice.
½ cup cherries, pitted.

Cherry-Lime Kefir Gelatin Directions:

1. Make plain water kefir and ferment it for 24 hours at room temperature.
2. Strain out the kefir grains.
3. Blend the cherries and add them to the fermenting vessel.
4. Store the kefir in the fridge overnight.
5. In the morning, strain the cherries out of the kefir.
6. Heat up the lime juice and stir the gelatin into it until it dissolves.

7. Let the lime juice and gelatin mixture cool until it reaches close to room temperature and stir the cherry-lime kefir into it. Add sugar, if necessary.
8. Pour the gelatin into a gelatin mold and place it in the fridge. It should solidify within a couple hours.

Apple Kefir

Apple kefir can be made with dried apples, fresh apples or apple juice. If you're using dried apples, they can be added before you ferment the kefir. If you're using fresh apples, it's best to wait until after the grains have been removed. Apple juice can be added before or after fermenting the kefir, but if you're adding it before, it's a good idea to make sure you have a spare set of grains handy. Fermenting in juice can be a bit hard on the grains.

Ingredients:

1 quart spring or mineral water.
¼ cup water kefir grains.
¼ cup of the sugar of your choice.
2 apples, peeled and cored.

Apple Kefir Directions:

1. Make plain water kefir and ferment it for 24 hours at room temperature. If you're using dried apples, add them before the ferment. Apple juice can be added now or in step 3.
2. Strain out the kefir grains.
3. If you're using fresh apples, peel them, core them and chop them up. Add them to the kefir and give it a good stir.
4. Store in an airtight container in the fridge. Strain the apples out of the kefir after a day or two.

Fizzy Apple Kefir Directions:

1. Follow steps 1 through 3 of the previous directions.
2. Place an airtight lid on the container and ferment the kefir at room temperature for an additional 12 to 24 hours.
3. Strain out the apples and move the kefir to the fridge once it's carbonated to your preference.

Strawberry Peach Kefir

There are two ways you can make strawberry peach kefir. You can either ferment the kefir using dried peaches for the first ferment or you can add fresh peaches once fermenting is complete and the grains have been strained out. The first method infuses the kefir with the light flavor of peaches, while the second brings the flavor of the peaches front and center.

If you're using fresh peaches, select peaches that are ripe, but haven't started to develop soft spots. They should be sweet, but not so sweet it's overpowering. Don't wait until your peaches are right on the verge of going bad before using them in water kefir.

Ingredients:

1 quart spring or mineral water.
¼ cup water kefir grains.
¼ cup of the sugar of your choice.
1 cup strawberries.
1 cup peaches.

Strawberry Peach Kefir Directions:

1. Make plain water kefir and ferment it for 24 hours at room temperature. If you're using dried peaches, add them to the kefir before you ferment it.
2. Strain out the kefir grains.

3. Blend the strawberries and add them to the fermenting vessel. If you're using fresh peaches, they can be blended and added now as well.
4. Store the kefir in an airtight container in the fridge. Strain the strawberries and peaches out of the kefir after a day or two.

Strawberry Peach Kefir Directions:

1. Follow steps 1 through 3 of the previous directions.
2. Place an airtight lid on the container and ferment it at room temperature for an additional 12 to 24 hours.
3. Move the kefir to the fridge once it's carbonated to your preference. Store it in an airtight container. Strain the strawberries and peaches out of the kefir after a day or two.

Berry Medley Kefir

I have multiple berry bushes growing in my yard and there are times when I have more berries than I know what to do with. Don't get me wrong, I love berries. I've just got to be creative and constantly come up with new ways to use them. This recipe came about as a result of having 4 different types of berries sitting on the counter at once and wanting to find a way to use them all. I threw all the berries in the water kefir jar with a batch of plain kefir I'd just fermented and left it overnight, not knowing exactly what to expect.

It turned out great and has become one of my go-to recipes during berry season. I like it better as plain berry kefir, while the rest of my family likes it carbonated.

Ingredients:

2 quarts spring or mineral water.
½ cup of the sugar of your choice.
½ cup water kefir grains.
1 cup strawberries, sliced.
½ cup blueberries.
½ cup blackberries.
½ cup raspberries.

Berry Medley Kefir Directions:

1. Make plain water kefir and ferment it for 24 hours at room temperature.
2. Strain out the kefir grains.

3. Add the berries to a blender and pulse a few times until coarsely chopped.
4. Stir the berries into the water kefir.
5. Store in an airtight container in the fridge. After a day or two in the fridge, strain the berries out of the kefir.

Fizzy Berry Medley Kefir Directions:

1. Follow steps 1 through 4 of the previous directions.
2. Place an airtight lid on the jar and ferment it at room temperature for an additional 24 hours.
3. Strain the berries out of the kefir and move it to the fridge once it's carbonated to your preference.

Pomegranate Fizz

I really don't care for this recipe after the first ferment, but add some carbonation via a second ferment and it becomes a pretty good facsimile to pomegranate soda.

Use fresh pomegranate when it available. When fresh pomegranates are out of season, Pom Wonderful juice can be substituted. It's one of the few fruit juices out there that's made of almost 100% juice.

Ingredients:

1 quart spring or mineral water.
¼ cup water kefir grains.
¼ cup of the sugar of your choice.
1 cup pomegranate seeds (or pomegranate juice)

Pomegranate Fizz Directions:

1. Make plain water kefir and ferment it for 24 hours at room temperature. Do not add the pomegranate before fermenting the kefir.
2. Strain out the kefir grains.
3. If using pomegranate seeds, place them in a blender and pulse until they're chopped up. Add the seeds to the jar. If using juice, pour the juice into the jar.
4. Stir the juice or seeds into the water kefir.
5. Place an airtight lid on the container and ferment it for an additional 24 to 48 hours.

6. Once the kefir is carbonated to your preference, strain the seeds out of the jar. Store the kefir in an airtight container in the fridge.

Grape Juice Kefir

Grape juice kefir is made by placing water kefir grains directly into organic grape juice. The acids in the grape juice can be a little tough on water kefir grains and the grains will be stained by the color of the grape juice, so it's a good idea to only use extra grains for this purpose.

If you do a long second ferment with this recipe, you'll end up with something similar in taste to champagne. Be aware the longer ferment will result in elevated alcohol levels, so use good judgment when giving grape juice kefir to children.

Ingredients:

1 quart organic grape juice.
¼ cup water kefir grains.

Grape Juice Kefir Directions:

1. Pour the grape juice into the jar and add the kefir grains. Stir the contents of the jar and cover the mouth with cheesecloth or a towel.
2. Secure the cover in place and ferment the grape juice at room temperature for up to 48 hours.
3. Strain out the kefir grains.
4. Store in an airtight container in the fridge.

Fizzy Grape Juice Kefir Directions:

1. Follow steps 1 through 3 of the previous directions.
2. Place an airtight lid on the jar and ferment it at room temperature for an additional 12 to 24 hours.
3. Off-gas the container and move it to the fridge once it's carbonated to your preference.

Tropical Sunrise Kefir

Anyone who's attempted to ferment pineapple juice can attest to the fact that it will cause kefir to get slimy. This bothered me for a long time because I've always wanted to include pineapple in my water kefir recipes. It seems like a natural fit for many plain water kefir and fizzy kefir recipes.

Then one day it hit me. Adding pineapple juice to kefir doesn't cause it to get slimy right away. It's a delayed reaction to one of the chemical compounds found in the pineapple. I realized then that pineapple juice can be added to kefir as long as you drink it right away. Whatever you do, don't try to store this recipe with the pineapple juice in it.

Add a shot of grenadine, a shot of spiced rum and a shot of triple sec to this recipe and you get a pretty good imitation of the alcoholic tropical sunrise recipe. I have no clue whether the added alcohol is bad for the probiotic bacteria, but I'm assuming it's probably OK since there's already at least some alcohol in water kefir after fermentation is complete.

Ingredients:

1 quart spring or mineral water.
¼ cup water kefir grains.
¼ cup of the sugar of your choice.
¼ cup orange juice.
3 tablespoons pineapple juice.

Cherries, for garnish.

Tropical Sunrise Kefir Directions:

1. Make plain water kefir and ferment it for 24 hours at room temperature.
2. Strain out the kefir grains.
3. Add the orange juice to the kefir and stir it in. Taste and add sugar, as needed.
4. Store in an airtight container in the fridge.
5. Add pineapple juice, to taste, to the kefir when you're ready to drink it and stir it in.
6. Garnish with a pitted cherry before serving. The tiny umbrellas are optional.

Fizzy Tropical Sunrise Kefir Directions:

1. Follow steps 1 through 3 of the previous directions.
2. Place an airtight lid on the container and ferment it at room temperature for an additional 12 to 24 hours.
3. Off-gas the container and move it to the fridge once it's carbonated to your preference.
4. Add pineapple juice, to taste, to the kefir when you're ready to drink it and stir it in.
5. Garnish with a pitted cherry before serving.

Coconut Pineapple Kefir

Coconut pineapple kefir is another recipe that adds pineapple to water kefir to create a tropical flavor. Add the pineapple juice right before you drink the kefir, so it doesn't have time to get slimy.

Ingredients:

1 quart spring or mineral water.
¼ cup water kefir grains.
¼ cup of the sugar of your choice.
¼ cup pineapple juice.
¼ cup shredded coconut.

Coconut Pineapple Kefir Directions:

1. Make plain water kefir and ferment it for 24 hours at room temperature.
2. Strain out the kefir grains.
3. Add the shredded coconut to the kefir.
4. Store it in an airtight container in the fridge.
5. Add pineapple juice, to taste, to the kefir when you're ready to drink it and stir it in.

Fizzy Coconut Pineapple Kefir Directions:

1. Follow steps 1 through 3 of the previous directions.

2. Place an airtight lid on the container and ferment it at room temperature for an additional 12 to 24 hours.

3. Off-gas the container and move it to the fridge once it's carbonated to your preference.

4. Add pineapple juice, to taste, to the kefir when you're ready to drink it and stir it in.

Coconut Melon Kefir

Coconut melon kefir uses coconut water instead of mineral or spring water. It then adds coconut flakes to it for a double burst of coconut flavor. The watermelon tops this recipe off nicely and gives it the light sweetness only watermelon has.

This recipe is good as both plain kefir and fizzy kefir. When making plain kefir, I like to ferment it a little bit longer than normal to give it a good tangy flavor. This isn't necessary when doing a second ferment because it'll get the tangy flavor during the ferment.

Ingredients:

1 quart coconut water.
¼ cup water kefir grains.
¼ cup of the sugar of your choice.
¼ cup coconut flakes.
1 cup watermelon juice.

Coconut Melon Directions:

1. Use the coconut water to make plain water kefir. Ferment it for 24 to 36 hours if you're planning on making plain kefir, but only 24 hours if you're planning on making fizzy kefir.
2. Strain out the kefir grains.
3. Add the shredded coconut and watermelon to the kefir and stir it in.
4. Store it in an airtight container in the fridge.

Fizzy Coconut Melon Kefir Directions:

1. Follow steps 1 through 3 of the previous directions.
2. Place an airtight lid on the container and ferment it at room temperature for an additional 12 to 24 hours.
3. Off-gas the container and move it to the fridge once it's carbonated to your preference. Store it in an airtight container.

Kefir Fruit Punch

Most people have never tasted fruit punch made with fresh fruits and juices. They've tried the commercial stuff with the artificial flavors and colors, but the real juices rarely make into the fruit punch found on store shelves—and when it does, there's only a tiny amount of fruit juice in the container.

That's one of the biggest reasons I swore off prepackaged juices and punches years ago. I started reading the labels closely and was shocked at how many of the beverages I thought were good for my family only contained 10% juice, not to mention all the other harmful ingredients they contain.

Ingredients:

1 quart spring or mineral water.
¼ cup water kefir grains.
¼ cup of the sugar of your choice.
¼ cup orange juice.
1 cup cherries, pitted.
1 cup peach slices.
10 strawberries.

Kefir Fruit Punch Directions:

1. Make plain water kefir and ferment it for 24 hours at room temperature.
2. Strain out the kefir grains.
3. Add the orange juice to the kefir and stir it in.

4. Place the cherries, peach slices and strawberries into a blender and blend until they're chopped up. Add the fruit to the kefir and stir it in.
5. Store in an airtight container in the fridge. Strain out the solids after a day or two.

Fizzy Kefir Fruit Punch Directions:

1. Follow steps 1 through 4 of the previous directions.
2. Place an airtight lid on the container and ferment it at room temperature for an additional 12 to 24 hours.
3. Strain the solids out of the fruit punch.
4. Off-gas the container and move it to the fridge once it's carbonated to your preference.

Carrot Kefir

In addition to the vegetables, herbs and spices that can be added to water kefir, there's the occasional vegetable that can also be used. Carrot juice is added to this recipe to create a kefir that's the perfect fit for those who prefer drinking vegetables to fruit.

This recipe is best after a single ferment. I can't think of any good reason to carbonate carrot kefir, but I'm sure it can be done if you want to try it.

Ingredients:

1 quart spring or mineral water.
¼ cup water kefir grains.
¼ cup of the sugar of your choice.
2 cups carrots.
1 tablespoon fresh lemon juice.
1 teaspoon ginger, grated.

Carrot Kefir Directions:

1. Make plain water kefir and ferment it for 24 hours at room temperature.
2. Strain out the kefir grains.
3. Place the carrots, lemon juice and ginger into a blender and pulse until the carrots are chopped into small pieces.
4. Add the mixture to the fermenting jar and stir it up.

5. Store in an airtight container in the fridge. Strain out the solids after a day or two.

Vanilla Cream Kefir

My favorite soda has always been vanilla cream soda. When I switched over to eating healthy, it was the unhealthy habit that took me the longest to kick because I kept putting it off. I couldn't imagine life without the comfort of vanilla cream. Then I discovered water kefir and realized I could make my own vanilla cream soda imitation that's fairly close to the real thing. I was able to give up vanilla cream soda and haven't looked back since.

Ingredients:

1 quart spring or mineral water.
¼ cup water kefir grains.
¼ cup of the sugar of your choice.
1 tablespoon vanilla extract.

Coconut milk, for serving.

Vanilla Cream Kefir Directions:

1. Make plain water kefir and ferment it for 24 hours at room temperature.
2. Strain out the kefir grains.
3. Add the vanilla and 2 additional tablespoons of sugar to the kefir and stir it in.
4. Place an airtight lid on the kefir and ferment it at room temperature for an additional 12 to 24 hours.

5. Transfer the kefir to cold storage once it has carbonated to your preference. Store it in an airtight container in the fridge.
6. Stir a tablespoon or two of coconut milk into the vanilla bean kefir right before you serve it for a creamier taste.

Orange Cream Kefir

As much as I used to enjoy vanilla cream soda, I really didn't care for soda of the orange cream variety. The orange flavor always seemed like it was shoehorned in between me and my beloved vanilla cream. I didn't think I would care for orange cream kefir either, but it surprised me. Maybe it's because fresh orange juice is used instead of artificial orange flavoring, or maybe it's just because it's kefir and I know it's good for me, but I find myself craving orange cream kefir from time to time.

Ingredients:

1 quart spring or mineral water.
¼ cup water kefir grains.
¼ cup of the sugar of your choice.
1 tablespoon vanilla extract.
¼ cup orange juice.

Coconut milk, for serving.

Orange Cream Kefir Directions:

1. Make plain water kefir and ferment it for 24 hours at room temperature.
2. Strain out the kefir grains.
3. Add the vanilla and 2 additional tablespoons of sugar to the kefir and stir it in. Add the orange juice and stir it in as well.

4. Place an airtight lid on the jar and ferment it at room temperature for an additional 12 to 24 hours.
5. Transfer the kefir to cold storage once it has carbonated to your preference. Store it in an airtight container in the fridge.
6. Stir a tablespoon or two of coconut milk into the vanilla bean kefir right before you serve it for a creamier taste.

Root Beer Kefir

Root beer kefir is another soda imitation that ends up being better than the real thing. When you use natural ingredients and real sugars instead of processed sugar, you end up with a root beer that's tough to beat. This recipe combines a lot of different flavorings to get a good root beer flavor. If you're looking for an easier way out, try using root beer extract. You'll end up with pretty good root beer kefir without all the hassle.

I'm all about eating healthy most of the time, but every once in a while you've got to reward yourself. If you really want to indulge, try this root beer with a scoop of homemade ice cream.

Ingredients:

1 quart spring or mineral water.
¼ cup water kefir grains.
½ cup of the sugar of your choice.
2 tablespoons molasses.
½ cup sassafras root bark.
1 tablespoon vanilla extract.
1 licorice root, chopped up.
1 cinnamon stick.
2 star anise heads.

Root Beer Kefir Directions:

1. Make plain water kefir and ferment it for 24 hours at room temperature.

2. Strain out the kefir grains.
3. Add all of the ingredients to the fermenting jar and stir them together.
4. Place an airtight lid on the jar and ferment it at room temperature for an additional 12 to 24 hours.
5. Transfer the kefir to cold storage once it has carbonated to your preference. Store it in an airtight container in the fridge.

Ginger Ale Kefir

Buy commercial ginger ale from the store and there's a fairly good chance you're going to end up purchasing a product that has little, if any, actual ginger in it. Oddly enough, many of the major manufacturers opt to completely leave the ginger out of ginger ale. Add that to the fact that many of them use high-fructose corn syrup, artificial flavors and preservatives and you're much better off making your own ginger ale at home.

Play around with the quantities of the ingredients in this recipe until you nail the flavor down just right. Don't be surprised if you end up liking natural ginger ale more than the commercial stuff. The ginger ale most people are accustomed to is a flavored imitation and pales in comparison to the real thing.

Ingredients:

1 quart spring or mineral water.
¼ cup water kefir grains.
¼ cup of the sugar of your choice.
2 tablespoons lemon juice.
1 tablespoon ginger, finely chopped
5 to 10 raisins.

Ginger Ale Kefir Directions:

1. Make plain water kefir and ferment it for 24 hours at room temperature. Add the lemon juice,

ginger and raisins to the kefir before fermenting it.

2. Strain out the kefir grains.

3. Place an airtight container on the jar and ferment it for an additional 24 to 48 hours.

4. Once the ginger ale kefir is carbonated to your preference, place a lid on it and store it in an airtight container in the fridge.

Green Tea Kefir

If you have extra grains lying around, try making the tea first and adding the water kefir grains directly to the tea. Those who only have a single set of grains will want to make plain water kefir and add the tea to it after the grains have been removed. The directions below are for fermenting prepared tea. If you want to add the tea after fermenting, make plain water kefir and remove the grains before cold-steeping the tea. I've found high-quality loose leaf tea works best for cold steeping. It's a bit more of a hassle to strain the leaves out of the tea once it's done steeping, but the added flavor is well-worth the extra effort.

Whatever you do, don't warm the tea up before you drink it. Too hot of tea will kill the probiotic bacteria and render the kefir ineffective. If you're planning on heating the tea, you might as well just make regular green tea without the ferment.

Don't bother with a second ferment with this recipe unless the idea of drinking green tea soda appeals to you. That's exactly what it tastes like and it isn't very appealing.

Ingredients:

1 quart spring or mineral water.
¼ cup water kefir grains.
¼ cup of the sugar of your choice.
2 tablespoons of loose leaf green tea.

Green Tea Kefir Directions:

1. Bring the water to a boil. Turn off the heat and add the tea leaves. Let them steep in the water for 15 minutes. Strain the tea leaves out of the tea. Stir the sugar into the tea while it's still hot.

2. Pour the tea into the fermenting jar. Once the tea has cooled to room temperature, add the water kefir grains to the jar and place a towel or piece of cheesecloth over the mouth of the jar. Secure it in place and leave the tea to ferment at room temperature for 16 to 24 hours.

3. Taste the tea and if it's too sweet, allow it to ferment for an additional 24 hours.

4. Strain out the grains.

5. Store the green tea kefir in an airtight container in the fridge.

Fermented Nettle Tea Kefir

I have an uncomfortable relationship with the nettle plant—literally. For some reason, no matter how much I cover up, I always get stung and end up with a rash. If nettle wasn't so darn good for you, I wouldn't bother, but it's really a great little weed. It has a bit of a prickly personality, but it's not bad once you get past the rough exterior.

While doing research for this book, I found out there are more than 500 varieties of nettle plants in existence (4). The type of nettle I'm talking about is the average, run-of-the-mill nettle plant found in backyards, parks and wilderness areas across most of the United States. I've heard there are areas of the United States that call other inedible plants nettles, so make sure you know exactly what you're eating before you eat it. I also can't guarantee that all 500 varieties of nettle are edible.

If you decide to go out and harvest nettle, you'll probably be the only person in the park who isn't avoiding the stuff like the plague. Make sure you wear long-sleeves, gloves and thick pants. Bring a pair of scissors, so you'll be able to snip leaves off with ease. The tender tops of the plants are the best for harvest. Snipping them off will cause nettle plants to spread out and you'll be able to harvest from the same plant throughout the season. Or you can skip the hassle and purchase your nettle online through Mountain Rose Herbs or another online retailer. You can purchase a pound of organic nettle for around $10.

Make sure you boil nettle before attempting to eat it or use it in a recipe. Boiling nettle eliminates the stinging chemical and makes it so it's edible. This recipe boils nettle for tea, but you can add a bit of butter to the boiled nettles and eat them, too. A single cup of nettles contains nearly half of your recommended daily allowance of calcium, a third of your vitamin A and a couple grams of natural protein. They're also packed full of vitamin K (5).

Ingredients:

1 quart spring or mineral water.
4 tablespoons of the sugar of your choice.
¼ cup water kefir grains.
2 cups of nettles.

Nettle Kefir Directions:

1. Bring the water to a boil and add the nettles. Boil them for 10 minutes.
2. Turn off the heat and let the nettles sit in the water for 45 minutes. You can leave them longer if you want stronger nettle tea.
3. Strain the nettle leaves out of the tea.
4. Stir the sugar into the tea and pour it into the jar. Add the water kefir grains to the jar and place a towel or piece of cheesecloth over the mouth. Secure it in place and leave the tea to ferment at room temperature for 24 hours.
5. Taste the tea and if it's still too sweet, allow it to ferment for up to 24 hours longer.
6. Strain out the grains. Move them to another batch of sugar water right away.

7. Store the nettle tea kefir in the fridge in an airtight container.

Hibiscus Ginger Kefir Cooler

When I tell people what's in this tasty recipe, I more often than not get blank stares and the reply, "You mean the flower?" Most people are familiar with hibiscus as a garden flower, but aren't aware it can be consumed and is said to have a number of health benefits. A number of studies have shown hibiscus to be an effective tool for both cholesterol and blood pressure maintenance. It's used in traditional medicine around the globe for everything from upper respiratory health to restlessness (6).

There may be some risk associated with drinking hibiscus tea. If you have low blood pressure or are taking medicine to regulate your blood pressure, it could cause your blood pressure to drop too low. It's known to interact with some medicines and may pose a risk to pregnant women (7).

This recipe is best when consumed as plain kefir and isn't a good option for a second ferment.

Ingredients:

1 quart spring or mineral water.
¼ cup of the sugar of your choice.
¼ cup water kefir grains.
½ cup dried hibiscus.
1 tablespoon ginger, grated.
2 tablespoons fresh lime juice.

Hibiscus Ginger Cooler Directions:

1. Make plain water kefir and ferment it for 24 hours at room temperature.
2. Strain out the kefir grains.
3. Stir the lime juice, dried hibiscus and ginger into the jar.
4. Store in an airtight container in the fridge. After a day or two, strain the solids out of the container.

Hibiscus Blueberry Kefir Cooler

If ginger isn't your thing, but you still want to try hibiscus, here's a recipe that mixes the flavors of hibiscus and blueberry together to create a cooler that's a great way to cool down on a hot summer day.

The hibiscus is boiled in this recipe to really infuse the flavor into the kefir. Since it's boiled, it has to be done prior to fermentation. I've done this a couple time with a set of back-up grains I keep handy and haven't had any problems with the grains yet. I'd suggest using back-up grains to make this beverage just to be on the safe side. Alternatively, the hibiscus can be added after the grains are removed, but you can't heat the kefir.

This recipe is equally good as a plain or fizzy kefir recipe.

Ingredients:

1 quart spring or mineral water.
¼ cup water kefir grains.
¼ cup of the sugar of your choice.
½ cup dried hibiscus.
1 cup fresh or frozen blueberries.

Hibiscus Blueberry Kefir Cooler Directions:

1. Bring the water to a boil. Add the dried hibiscus and turn off the heat. Let the hibiscus steep until the water has cooled.
2. Pour the hibiscus tea into the fermenting jar.

3. Add the grains to the jar and stir the contents. Place a loose lid onto the jar and let it ferment at room temperature for 24 hours.
4. Strain out the kefir grains.
5. Muddle the blueberries and add them to the jar.
6. Store in an airtight container in the fridge. Strain out the solids after a day or two.

Fizzy Hibiscus Blueberry Kefir Cooler Directions:

1. Follow steps 1 through 5 of the previous directions.
2. Place an airtight lid on the jar and ferment for an additional 12 to 24 hours.
3. Strain the solids out of the kefir.
4. Off-gas the container and move it to the fridge.

Lavender Lemonade Kefir

This is another recipe that integrates flower petals into water kefir. This time lavender is paired with lemons to craft a kefir that's light and refreshing and is, in my opinion, one of the best recipes in the book.

If you've never used lavender before, there's one thing you need to keep in mind. More is not better when it comes to lavender. Beverages that use lavender can quickly go from being infused with the delicious light flavor of lavender to something that tastes similar to what drinking perfume would probably taste like. Start with just a little and gradually add more until you reach your comfort zone.

Ingredients:

1 quart spring or mineral water.
¼ cup of the sugar of your choice.
¼ cup water kefir grains.
¼ cup fresh lemon juice.
1 to 2 teaspoons lavender petals.

Lavender Lemonade Kefir Directions:

1. Make plain water kefir and ferment it for 24 hours at room temperature.
2. Strain out the kefir grains.
3. Add the lavender and lemon juice to the kefir.
4. Store it in an airtight container in the fridge. After a day or two in the fridge, strain the solids out of the kefir.

Fizzy Lavender Lemonade Kefir Directions:

1. Follow steps 1 through 3 of the previous directions.
2. Place an airtight lid on the jar and ferment it at room temperature for an additional 24 hours.
3. Strain the solids out of the kefir and move it to the fridge once it's carbonated to your preference.

Chia Seed Kefir

Remember when we were younger and Chia Pets were all the craze? You took the seeds and grew them on an animal-shaped mold and it looked like it had green fur. I had one when I was a kid, as I'm sure many of you did, too. Who would have thought then that those seeds aren't just edible, but are actually good for you?

When you add chia seeds to water kefir and leave it overnight, the seeds enlarge and become gel-like. I don't care much for the way they taste on their own, but some people do. Try it, and even if you don't like it by itself, this recipe makes a great addition to smoothies and other dishes that call for chia seeds.

Ingredients:

1 quart spring or mineral water.
¼ cup water kefir grains.
¼ cup of the sugar of your choice.
2 cups chia seeds.

Chia Seed Kefir Directions:

1. Make plain water kefir and ferment it for 24 hours at room temperature.
2. Strain out the kefir grains.
3. Pour the chia seeds into a quart-sized jar and add enough water kefir to the jar to cover the top of the seeds.

4. Place the jar into the refrigerator and leave it overnight. The seeds should expand and be ready to eat by the morning.

Immunity Boost Kefir

This recipe is packed full of fruit containing vitamin C. I start drinking it at the first sign of a cold or sore throat and it seems to relieve the symptoms and may even lessen the duration of the illness. Both the blueberries and the oranges are packed full of vitamin C.

Rose hips are an ingredient you may not be familiar with. They're the fruit of the rose plant, usually the wild dog rose. They contain 50% more vitamin C than oranges do in addition to a number of antioxidant compounds believed to boost the immune system (8).

Ingredients:

1 quart spring or mineral water.
¼ cup of the sugar of your choice.
¼ cup water kefir grains.
½ cup blueberries.
¼ cup fresh orange juice.
1 tablespoon dried rosehips.

Immunity Boost Kefir Directions:

1. Make plain water kefir and ferment it for 24 hours at room temperature.
2. Strain out the kefir grains.
3. Add the berries to a blender and pulse a few times until coarsely chopped.
4. Stir the berries, orange juice and rosehips into the kefir.

5. Store it in an airtight container in the fridge. After a day or two in the fridge, strain the solids out of the container.

Fizzy Immunity Boost Kefir Directions:

1. Follow steps 1 through 4 of the previous directions.
2. Place an airtight lid on the jar and ferment it at room temperature for an additional 24 hours.
3. Strain the solids out of the kefir and move it to the fridge once it's carbonated to your preference.

Frozen Water Kefir Fruit Pops

Who said desserts have to be unhealthy to be good? Freezing water kefir doesn't kill off the probiotic bacteria, which means it can be used to make tasty probiotic desserts. This recipe uses nothing more than plain water kefir and chopped fruit to create a frozen fruit pop that's delicious and healthy.

Feel free to play around with the kinds of fruit you use in the pops. This recipe is one of my favorite, but I've been known to throw whatever's in season at the time into the popsicle molds.

Ingredients:

1 quart spring or mineral water.
¼ cup water kefir grains.
¼ cup of the sugar of your choice.
1 cup raspberries.
2 cups sliced strawberries.
1 cup red seedless grapes, sliced in half.
1 cup blackberries.
¼ cup shredded coconut.

Frozen Water Kefir Fruit Pops Directions:

1. Make plain water kefir and ferment it for 24 hours at room temperature.
2. Strain out the kefir grains.
3. Prepare the fruit and divide it amongst your popsicle molds.

4. Pour water kefir into the molds. Add the popsicle stick to each mold and put it in the freezer.
5. Freeze for at least 6 hours.
6. Enjoy.

Watermelon Granita Kefir

Granitas are similar to sorbets, except they're churned by hand and require a little extra effort. The reward is a delicious frozen dessert with a coarse, flaky texture. The key to making the perfect granita is frequent scrapings that break up the ice crystals as they're starting to form. Forget to stir your granita a couple times and you'll end up with a solid block of frozen liquid instead of the dessert you were hoping for. If this happens, you can still scrape it; it's just going to take a bit more effort on your part.

Ingredients:

1 cup fizzy water kefir.
10 cups of seedless watermelon chunks.
4 tablespoons fresh lime juice.
½ cup sugar.

Watermelon Granita Directions:

1. Add all of the ingredients to a blender or food processor and blend until smooth. You'll probably have to do this in batches.
2. Pour the mixture into a 9" X 13" baking dish and place the baking dish into the freezer.
3. Leave the dish in the freezer for a couple hours, until a light layer of ice has formed on the top. Use a spoon or a fork to scrape the top layer of ice away from the softer granita below it. Once

you get down to the granita that isn't frozen, place the dish back into the freezer.

4. Wait another hour or two and scrape it again.

5. Repeat this process until you reach the bottom of the dish. You should be left with a light, fluffy frozen dessert.

Kefir Applesauce

I'm a big fan of applesauce, but I'm not keen on the prepared applesauce you can buy at the store because of the high-fructose corn syrup, artificial coloring and other questionable ingredients found in some of the applesauce brands out there, not to mention the chemicals and pesticides used on the apples while they're growing. One of my biggest pet peeves is manufacturers that take foods that should be healthy and turn them into abominations.

This applesauce uses a small handful of ingredients and is completely natural, as long as you use a natural sugar to make the water kefir. It's simple and healthy, which is exactly what applesauce should be.

Whatever you do, don't can this applesauce or otherwise heat it up. The heat used in the canning process will kill the probiotic bacteria in the kefir. You'll still have applesauce, but it won't contain any of the beneficial bacteria from the kefir that was added. If you want to preserve this applesauce, store it in the freezer.

Ingredients:

10 apples.
½ cup plain water kefir.
2 tablespoons cinnamon.

Kefir Applesauce Directions:

1. Peel, core and chop up the apples.

2. Add the apples to a blender or food processor and blend until smooth.
3. Add the cinnamon and blend it in.
4. Store in airtight containers in the fridge or the freezer.

Preserving Vegetables With Water Kefir

In the first book in this series, we briefly mentioned using water kefir grains as a starter culture for vegetable ferments. Kefir grains contain at least some of the same lactobacteria found in fermented vegetables, so they can be used in most vegetable ferments. The probiotic profile of vegetables fermented with water kefir grains will be similar to those fermented using traditional methods, but there will be at least some different strains of lactobacteria and yeasts in the container.

Fermenting vegetables allows you to preserve them and put them away, so you can preserve the harvest. You're able to take full advantage of the good prices that are around when vegetables are in-season locally and can ferment a bunch of vegetables to ensure you'll have them well into the off-season.

Using water kefir grains to ferment vegetables may damage the grains, so they're usually left in the vegetables and can be blended up and consumed as part of the dish. It's a great way to use up extra grains that have grown and you don't know what to do with them. You may find you're able to ferment multiple batches of vegetables with the same grains, but I've tried it and have noticed the second batch of vegetables isn't as robust as the first.

When adding water kefir grains to vegetables in order to ferment them, you may be able to reduce the amount of salt that's required in the recipe. I don't recommend reducing it too much because the salt helps prevent bad bacteria from growing in the initial stages of the ferment and may prevent mold growth.

Unlike water kefir ferments, vegetable ferments should be done in an anaerobic environment using either a container with an airtight lid or an airlock container. Make sure the vegetables stay submerged beneath the brine the entire time they're fermenting. Allowing them to come into contact with air may allow mold or other harmful pathogens to grow.

Kefir Cultured Sauerkraut

Here's an interesting way to use up extra grains you have laying around—use them to ferment sauerkraut. Kefir cultured sauerkraut is almost indistinguishable from regular sauerkraut when it comes to flavor and texture.

Blend the grains up before using them in this recipe. They can be stirred into the sauerkraut and eaten as part of the recipe.

Ingredients:

1 head of cabbage.
1 tablespoon sugar.
2 tablespoons salt.
5 tablespoons water kefir grains.

Kefir Cultured Sauerkraut Directions:

1. Wash the cabbage. Peel off the outer leaves, core it and chop it into small strips. Add the cabbage to a large bowl and the salt to the bowl.
2. Use a kraut pounder (or any blunt object) to bruise the cabbage. This will cause it to release its natural juices. Add the sugar to the cabbage and stir it in once you've pounded all the cabbage. This will provide food for your grains.
3. Add 2 ½ tablespoons of water kefir grains to the bottom of the fermenting jar.
4. Place half of the cabbage into the jar. Compress the cabbage tightly.

5. Add the rest of the water kefir grains to the jar. Place the remaining cabbage over the top and compress it tightly.

6. Add a weight to the jar. The weight can be anything made from a non-porous and non-reactive material that fits snugly into the jar. Glass and smooth stone weights work well. In a pinch, you can use a plastic baggie filled with small stones. Place the weight into the jar and press it down until it's holding the cabbage beneath the surface of the liquid in the jar.

7. If the cabbage didn't release enough liquid, add water to the jar until the cabbage is submerged.

8. Seal the jar so it's airtight and let it sit at room temperature for 3 to 4 days. Move it to the fridge when it's ready.

Kefir Cultured Dilly Carrots

Fermented carrots are another easy kefir grain ferment. They take about a week at room temperature to properly ferment, so plan accordingly. This dilly carrot recipe is a traditional fermented carrot recipe eaten in the United States.

Ingredients:

8 medium carrots.
4 cups filtered water.
2 tablespoons salt.
3 tablespoons water kefir grains.

Kefir Cultured Carrots Directions:

1. Wash the carrots. Peel them and chop them into sticks.
2. Add the water kefir grains to the bottom of the fermenting jar.
3. Place the carrots into the jar and ensure there are no air bubbles.
4. Combine the water and salt to create brine. Pour the brine over the carrots until the carrots are completely covered.
5. Add a weight to the jar and press it down until it's holding the carrots beneath the surface of the liquid in the jar.
6. If there isn't enough brine, add brine until the carrots are completely covered.

7. Seal the jar so it's airtight and let it sit at room temperature for 5 to 7 days. Start checking it after the 5th day and move it to the fridge when it's ready.

Kefir Cultured Dilly Beans

Fermented green beans are a traditional treat consumed by folks across the entire Midwest region of the United States. Now, thanks to the Internet and a handful of books containing dilly bean recipes, they've made their way across much of the world.

Ingredients:

3 cups green beans.
2 garlic cloves.
2 tablespoons fresh dill leaves.
1 tablespoon dill seeds.
3 tablespoons sea salt.
4 cups mineral or spring water.
2 tablespoons water kefir grains.

Kefir Cultured Carrots Directions:

1. Wash the green beans. Snap or cut off the ends and discard them. Place the green beans into the fermenting jar.
2. Add the water kefir grains to the jar.
3. Combine the water and salt to create brine. Pour the brine over the green beans until they're completely covered. Add the dill leaves, dill seeds and garlic cloves.
4. Add a weight to the jar and press it down until it's holding the green beans beneath the surface of the brine.

5. If there isn't enough brine, add brine until the green beans are completely covered.
6. Seal the jar so it's airtight and let it sit at room temperature for up to 5 days. Start checking it after the 3rd day and move it to the fridge when it's ready.

Kefired Cucumber Salad

This recipe is a great snack when you're looking for something light to hold you over until your next meal. It's also a good choice for those looking to add a probiotic side dish to a meal.

Ingredients:

4 medium cucumbers, peeled and sliced.
1 green bell pepper, sliced.
1 red bell pepper, sliced.
1 medium onion, chopped
2 tablespoons sea salt.
4 cups mineral or spring water.
2 tablespoons water kefir seeds.

Instructions:

1. Prepare the vegetables and add them to the fermenting jar.
2. Create brine by combining 4 cups of water with 2 tablespoons of sea salt.
3. Fill the jar with brine. Leave room for the weight. Get rid of any air bubbles that form in the jar.
4. Add the kefir grains to the fermenting jar.
5. Place the weight into the vessel and press it down. Make sure the weight is holding the vegetables beneath the surface of the brine.
6. Place the lid on the container and seal it so it's airtight.

7. Ferment at room temperature for up to 3 days. Check the vegetables daily and move them to cold storage once they've fermented to your preference.

Kefir Cauliflower

This recipe can be made without the curry powder if you don't like the spices. It'll be a bit bland, so feel free to add your own spice blend to the recipe. Most spices you'd normally use with vegetables can be used with this recipe.

Make sure you pick fresh cauliflower heads that are in prime eating condition when selecting the cauliflower for this recipe.

Ingredients:

2 heads of cauliflower, broken up into smaller florets.
3 garlic cloves, minces.
3 tablespoons curry powder.
2 tablespoons sea salt.
4 cups mineral or spring water.
2 tablespoons water kefir grains.

Instructions:

1. Prepare the vegetables and add them to the fermenting container.
2. Create brine by mixing the water and salt.
3. Fill the vessel with brine. Make sure the vegetables are covered.
4. Press the weight down into the vessel until the brine is over the top of the vegetables.
5. Seal the container so that it's airtight.
6. Ferment the cauliflower at room temperature until it has fermented to your preference.
7. Let the cauliflower ferment for 3 to 5 days, or until it has fermented to your liking and move it

to the fridge. Putting it into cold storage will slow down the fermentation process.

Frequently Asked Questions

If you're having trouble with your grains or have questions about the fermenting process, check this chapter first. It answers a lot of the most common questions people have in regards to fermenting water kefir.

What If There Aren't Any Bubbles In the Kefir?

Bubbles are just one of the many signs fermentation is taking place. While a lot of bubbles are a good indicator fermentation is taking place, the lack of bubbles doesn't always mean trouble. Some ferments produce bubbles at such a slow pace you'd have to sit there and stare at the fermenting jar for a long time to see them.

How Can I Tell If Fermentation Is Taking Place?

There are a number of signs you can look for that indicate fermentation is occurring. The most obvious sign is carbon dioxide gas bubbles rising to the surface. If there aren't any bubbles, you'll have to look for more subtle signs. The kefir won't be as sweet as it was when you started fermenting it, will take on a tangy flavor and the color of the water may change.

Why Did My Grains Change Color?

Water kefir grains can change color for a number of reasons. Unhealthy grains may take on a yellowish hue, especially if they've been fed sporadically. Changes to the grain color don't always mean something is amiss, as water kefir grains can take on the color of the liquids they're fermented in. This is especially true when the grains are used to ferment deep-colored liquids like grape juice.

Why Does My Kefir Taste Like Bad Wine?

This usually occurs when water kefir has been fermented for too long and is especially prominent after a long second ferment. Try shortening the length of time the kefir is fermented to see if that solves the problem.

How Can I Tell If My Grains Are Healthy?

Water kefir grains are generally pretty tough. As long as you keep them fed, they theoretically should stay healthy for quite some time. The only easy way to tell if your grains are healthy is to attempt to ferment a batch of water kefir with the grains. If they do a good job, it's highly likely your grains are in good health. On the other hand, grains that struggle to produce kefir may be in poor health and will need more frequent feedings and possibly more minerals in the water they're fermenting.

Can I Break My Grains Apart?

Healthy kefir grains can grow to large sizes, which makes them unwieldy and difficult to handle. If your grains get too large, they can be broken up or chopped up and the grains will be no worse for wear. In fact, it might actually benefit the grains to break them up because more of the surface area of the grains will be exposed to the liquid.

Why Are Some of My Grains Floating?

The most common reason grains float is because carbon dioxide bubbles have attached themselves to the grains and made them buoyant. This is natural and the grains will sink back down to the bottom of the container once fermentation slows down a bit. Damaged grains or freezer-burnt grains may also float. If your grains aren't producing good kefir and look like they have a hard crust on them, it may be time to replace them. Try breaking crusted grains apart if you suspect the crust may be preventing the bacteria inside the grains from properly fermenting kefir.

I Dropped My Grains on the Floor. Are They Still Good?

Probably. Wash them off under cool water and gently scrub the surface of the grains with your fingers. If you have backup grains and aren't sure about whether you want to add dropped grains back to your kefir, you can add them to smoothies and eat them.

Additional Reading

Book 1 in this series is on Fermented Vegetables. It can be purchased at the following location:

http://www.amazon.com/Fermented-Foods-vol-Vegetables-Preservation/dp/1499224834

Book 2 in the series covers milk kefir:

http://www.amazon.com/Fermented-Foods-vol-Kefir-Preservation-ebook/dp/B00K0T36QQ

Works Cited

1. **Unknown.** FAQ: Water Kefir Intro. *Yemoos Nourishing Cultures.* [Online] [Cited: 4-23, 2014.] http://www.yemoos.com/faqwaintro.html.

2. *The microbial diversity of water kefir.* **Gulitz, A, et al., et al.** 3, s.l. : Int J Food Microbiol, Vol. 151.

3. **Unknown.** Microbiome: Your Body Houses 10X More Bacteria Than Cells. *Discover Magazine.* [Online] [Cited: 4-12, 2014.] http://discovermagazine.com/galleries/zen-photo/m/microbiome.

4. **Staff, Mother Earth News.** The Many Stinging Nettle Benefits. *Mother Earth News.* [Online] 1981. [Cited: 3-24, 2014.]

5. **Unknown.** Nutritional Info: Stinging Nettles, blanched (Northern Plains Indians). *Skip the Pie.* [Online] [Cited: 2-12, 2014.] http://skipthepie.org/ethnic-foods/stinging-nettles-blanched-northern-plains-indians/.

6. **Hudson, Tori.** The Surprising Health Benefits of Hibiscus. *Gaia Herbs.* [Online] 7-9, 2013. [Cited: 4-21, 2014.] http://www.gaiaherbs.com/articles/detail/42/The-Surprising-Health-Benefits-of-Hibiscus.

7. **Anding, Roberta.** Risks of Hibiscus Tea. *SF Gate.* [Online] [Cited: 3-4, 2014.] http://healthyeating.sfgate.com/risks-drinking-hibiscus-tea-9953.html.

8. **Unknown.** Rose Hips. *Herb Wisdom.* [Online] [Cited: 5-2, 2014.] http://www.herbwisdom.com/herb-rose-hip.html.

Printed in Great Britain
by Amazon.co.uk, Ltd.,
Marston Gate.